MOUNTAIN HORROR

MOUNTAIN HORROR

by Anthony Masters
Illustrated by Ian Heard

FRANKLIN WATTS
LONDON•SYDNEY

Editor-in-Chief John C. Miles
Designer Jason Billin/Billin Design Solutions
Art Director Jonathan Hair

Cover artwork by Mark Bergin

© 2000 Anthony Masters

The right of Anthony Masters
to be identified as the author
of this work has been asserted by him.

First published in 2000
by Franklin Watts
96 Leonard Street
London
EC2A 4XD

Franklin Watts Australia
56 O'Riordan Street
Alexandria
NSW 2015

ISBN 0 7496 3723 4 (hbk)
        0 7496 4006 5 (pbk)

Dewey classification: 796.5

A CIP catalogue record for this book is available
from the British Library.

Printed in Great Britain

CONTENTS

THE STORM

◼ CHAPTER ONE

'Keep it together. Keep it together,' Jon muttered, over and over again.

This part of the journey down from the summit of Mount Everest was very difficult. Patches of loose pebbles were covered in 15 cm of fresh snow.

The descent had been terrifying and Jon still needed to keep his mind on the job.

'Keep it together,' Jon repeated.
'I've got to keep it together.'

Jon Krakauer, journalist and experienced climber, had paid to join an amateur expedition run by professional guides. The aim was to reach the summit of Everest.

On May 9th, 1996, five separate expeditions had begun the climb. At first the weather seemed perfect. Twenty-four hours later a fierce storm blew up.

As a result, a couple of dozen inexperienced climbers had to face the most dangerous moments of their lives. In the end, eight of them died. It was the worst tragedy Everest had ever known.

Disaster struck on the way down when the expeditions were caught in sub-zero temperatures. There is very little oxygen in the air at 8,000 metres. The area at this height is known to experienced climbers as 'The Death Zone'.

About twenty metres below the summit, Jon had noticed wispy clouds were filling the valley to the south. They covered all but the highest peaks.

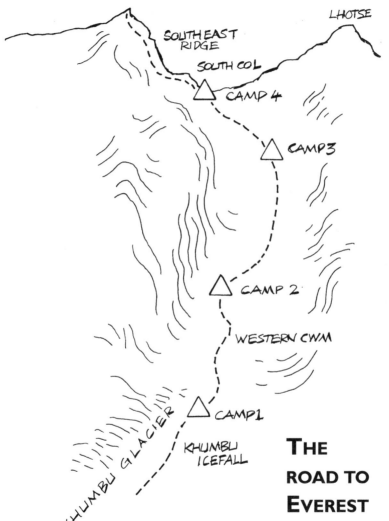

MOUNT EVEREST

LHOTSE

SOUTH EAST
RIDGE

SOUTH COL

△ CAMP 4

△ CAMP 3

△ CAMP 2

WESTERN CWM

△ CAMP 1

KHUMBU GLACIER

KHUMBU
ICEFALL

THE ROAD TO EVEREST

One of his fellow climbers was an experienced aircraft pilot. He later told Jon that those innocent-looking wisps of water vapour were the tops of powerful thunderhead clouds. A violent storm was on its way.

■ CHAPTER TWO

Soon after leaving the summit of
Everest, Jon reached a part of the
mountain known as the Hillary Step.
But his path was blocked by a group
of climbers going up on a single rope
and he had to wait.

Andy, who was one of the guides
in Jon's own group, joined him.

Andy was having breathing problems. He asked Jon to check the intake valve to his oxygen supply as he thought it must have iced up. Andy was right. Jon soon found that a large piece of frozen snot had blocked the rubber valve. He chipped it off with the pick of his ice axe.

Jon asked Andy to turn off his own regulator. This meant he could save oxygen while waiting for the other climbers to get out of the way. But Andy made the mistake of opening the valve rather than closing it.

As a result, ten minutes later, Jon's oxygen had been used up. He began to feel very spaced out in the thin air. Luckily, he managed to get another oxygen bottle.

Jon struggled on down. He still felt punch-drunk and kept repeating, 'Keep it together.'

Jon was worried that he would be unable to keep his mind on what he was doing. If he didn't he might begin to lose all sense of where he was. He could then plunge to his death.

Feeling very tired, Jon sat down to rest on a broad, sloping ledge. Suddenly a terrifying booming sound made him stand up again.

CHAPTER THREE

At first, Jon thought the booming must be an avalanche. But when he looked round at the slopes of Everest he could not see any sign of one. Then there was another booming sound and the sky was lit by a flash of lightning. Jon realised he had been hearing claps of thunder. The storm had arrived, and with it a severe blizzard.

As he climbed the mountain Jon had picked out landmarks that would guide him on the way down. This was a habit he had got into over years of climbing.

He would memorise the route. 'Remember to turn left at the buttress that looks like a ship's prow,' he would tell himself, or 'Follow that skinny line of snow until it curves sharply to the right.'

By 6.00 pm the blizzard was at full force, with driving snow and wind gusting at more than 60 knots an hour.

Luckily, Jon came across a rope that had been fixed by another expedition. Wrapping it around his arms, he carried on through the howling blizzard. Soon he had left the most difficult section of Everest behind him. He felt deeply relieved.

But his good luck wasn't to last. Suddenly Jon began to feel as if he couldn't breathe. To his horror he realised that his oxygen supply was running out again.

Earlier Jon had noticed that the bottle was only half full. But he had decided there was enough oxygen to get him down the mountain. He had taken much longer because of the storm. Now his oxygen had run out.

CHAPTER FOUR

Jon pulled the mask from his face and left it hanging round his neck. It was useless now. But he didn't feel worried about the danger. He had already had so many shocks that his mind had blotted out this last one.

Without oxygen, Jon had to take more rests. He was moving much more slowly. Soon he began to see strange things.

At first Jon felt as if he was looking down at his body from the sky. He imagined he was wearing a green cardigan. He also felt warm, despite the fact that the wind-chill factor was

in excess of seventy degrees
below zero.

By about 6.30 pm, Jon's fear
returned. Camp Four was visible
below him. There his tent and
warmth and safety waited. But there
was a final problem which might
prove fatal.

Jon saw below him a hard, glassy ice slope which he would have to cross without a rope. Snow pellets stung his face, hurled at him by the 70-knot gusts of wind. They were very painful. Any exposed flesh was immediately frozen.

CHAPTER FIVE

He sat down in the freezing blizzard,
trying to work out how he was going
to get down. One slip and he knew
he'd be dead. But he couldn't make
a decision. Jon spent the next forty-
five minutes with his mind drifting
like the snow.

Jon had to get himself going. He
had to make decisions. Above all he
needed a plan.

If he slipped off the icy slope he
would die at once. But that would be
better than dying slowly up here.

Jon stood up. He loved life too
much to throw it away. He could

dimly see the tents. He had to tackle this last danger and get back somehow.

He tightened up the ties of his hood until there was only a very small opening around his eyes. He then took off the useless and frozen-up oxygen mask.

Jon was just about to start down the slope when Andy suddenly appeared. Jon was horrified at the state of his face. In the light of his headlamp he could see Andy's cheeks were covered in frost.

One eye was frozen shut.

When he spoke, his words were badly slurred. 'Which way to the tents?' Andy gasped.

Jon pointed to Camp Four. Andy lurched towards the slope. He looked as if he was about to go tobogganing.

'It's steeper than it looks!' Jon yelled, above the noise of the storm.

■ CHAPTER SIX

Andy didn't seem to hear him. He was already sliding down the first and steepest part of the slope.

A few seconds later, Andy lost control and flipped over. Then he began to slide again, head-first down the ice at high speed.

Jon gazed down, just able to see Andy's body in the snow. It wasn't moving. Then, to his amazement, he saw him get up and wave casually. It was a miracle. Andy was now stumbling towards the tents.

Suddenly the blizzard eased up a little and Jon could see some figures standing outside the tents. Andy was still walking towards them as poor weather closed in yet again.

Jon lost his temper. Andy was a guide and should have waited for him. But at least he had given Jon some hope. If Andy could survive the slide then at least Jon would be in with a chance.

First of all, he decided to get rid of

his back-pack. It wasn't very heavy, but Jon was so tired he needed to get rid of any extra weight. He threw the pack over the edge and hoped it would land near the tents.

Slowly, he began to inch his way down the ice. Every step was terrifying.

When he finally made the bottom of the slope, he couldn't believe he was safe at last.

■ CHAPTER SEVEN

Jon picked up his pack and headed for his tent. He opened the flap and pulled himself in. Then he zipped the door shut and sank down. He was so tired that he couldn't sit upright. But at least he had made it back.

Jon lay there thinking about Andy. He realised now that he must have been light-headed from lack of oxygen and didn't know it was him. Andy would never have left him behind otherwise. At least he too was safe.

Jon suddenly felt a sense of deep satisfaction. He had actually climbed Everest in the worst possible weather.

He closed his eyes and fell into a deep sleep.

Many hours later, Jon Krakauer discovered that nineteen climbers were still stranded on Everest, fighting for their lives in the storm.

THE ICE PALACE

▨ CHAPTER ONE

Joe Simpson swung in a harness on the end of a rope in the crevasse. He had no idea how far down he had fallen.

He had thought that his climbing partner, Simon Yates, would have rescued him a long time ago. But slowly, painfully, Joe was beginning to realise that Simon must believe he was dead.

They were climbing in the Peruvian Andes in the late 1980s and Joe had broken his leg. Simon had been wonderful, letting him down the mountain in a roped harness.

But then Joe had fallen into the deep crevasse.

He continued to wait, praying that Simon would reappear and help him.

But in the back of his mind, Joe knew that Simon must have given up and gone back to base.

He would have to get out of the crevasse on his own – with a broken leg. The full hopelessness of it all came home to him.

Joe stared up at the bridge of ice across the crevasse and then gazed down at the drop below. He would never be able to climb up. He would have to go down. Although he was a highly experienced climber, Joe felt he couldn't move. He remembered feeling like this once before when he had been on a high diving board at a swimming pool.

Joe had gazed down at the water, willing himself to leap off into space.

But he had been terrified that the pool might suddenly move to one side and he would land on the ground. Or that the water would drain out as he dived and he would hit the bottom of the pool.

Using all his courage and willpower, Joe slowly let himself down the crevasse. He wanted to cry like a frightened child.

Joe hung shakily on the rope. His helmet was pressed to the ice wall and his eyes were tightly closed against the horror of it all.

▨ CHAPTER TWO

Joe forced his eyes open and gazed up at the rope that was still hanging from the ice bridge. He was terrified. Joe knew he had no hope of getting back up there. He studied the wall of the crevasse that was close to his shoulder. Opposite him, about three metres away, another wall rose up. Joe realised he was hanging in a shaft of watery ice.

As he turned, he swung round too quickly, catching his broken leg on the wall. He screamed with pain. Looking down, expecting to see the rope falling away into nothing, Joe saw a snow-covered floor. It was about five metres below him.

With a rush of relief, he knew he had made a mistake. He was not in as much danger as he had thought. Instead of hanging in some deep space, he was almost at the bottom of the crevasse!

Then Joe checked again and all his fears returned. There were dark holes in the snow floor and Joe realised he was really looking at a snow ceiling, not the bottom of the crevasse.

Joe then noticed that the walls opposite him closed but didn't quite meet. A narrow gap had been filled with snow to form a cone that rose right up to the ceiling.

The most amazing golden sunlight beamed down from a small hole in the roof. Sudden hope filled him. If only he could keep calm and work out a plan, he might get out of the trap.

Joe let himself slide down the rest of the rope, wanting to stand in the sunlight. He felt the beam was almost magical. It filled him with confidence.

Joe sat in his harness above the snow that he had once thought was a solid floor. Now he knew he was right. It was definitely a suspended ceiling across the crevasse.

The snow slope started running up to the sunshine about twelve metres away from him. Could he crawl across to it on the suspended ceiling, or would it collapse? Should he go straight across or keep as near as he could to the back wall of the crevasse? Either way, he could fall and simply swing in his harness. It could take a long time to die.

▨ CHAPTER THREE

Joe gazed again at the beam of sunlight. He decided to make the most direct approach. He would cross the middle of the snow ceiling.

Joe lowered himself down even further. He held his breath, every muscle tense. Soon he was sitting on the suspended ceiling with all his weight. But it was holding.

Joe sat very still for the next five minutes. He was trying to get used to the idea of being on a thin covering of snow above a huge drop. Would it hold? Could it hold? He had to try it out – and now!

If he didn't, he would be frozen with fear as well as with cold.

Joe let out about twelve metres of rope and tied the remaining nine metres to his harness.

Then he began to wriggle across the snow ceiling to the slope. Joe held his breath, his heart beating painfully.

CHAPTER FOUR

Once Joe had reached the halfway point he was sure the surface he was crawling over was strong enough.

After ten minutes or so, Joe lay against the slope which rose towards the golden sun in the roof of the crevasse.

Looking up he could see the climb would be much longer than he had supposed. If he slipped and fell, he would crash through the snow ceiling and plunge into the drop below. His rope would swing him into the ice wall.

For a moment Joe considered

climbing without the rope. Then if he
did fall his death would be mercifully
quick. But he dismissed the idea –
the rope gave him confidence.

Joe stood up cautiously on his left leg. He guessed the slope was about forty metres high. He could have climbed it in about ten minutes with two good legs. But how was he going to climb with one?

The slope was at an angle of forty-five degrees.

Joe hoped he could somehow drag himself up, but as he got higher he found the angle increased until the top six metres looked almost vertical.

The first part of the climb was incredibly frightening. He felt very clumsy, trying to use his left leg and drag his broken right leg behind him.

Joe dug his ice axe as deep as he could into the snow above him. He then pulled himself up with his arms. Luckily they were very strong. If the axe came out, he knew he would fall and swing on the rope for ever. Joe decided to stop. He must try and work out a better technique.

His whole body was shaking, and now his knee was throbbing badly.

■ CHAPTER FIVE

Joe tried lifting up his injured leg so
that it was on the same level as his
good one. Immediately he felt the
most terrible pain. His smashed knee
refused to bend.

Joe leant down and dug a step in
the snow. Then he dug another step
below it. He planted both his axes in
the snow above, got ready for more
pain and heaved his bad leg up until
the boot rested in the lower step.
Bracing himself on the axes, he
hopped with his good leg. At the
same time he pushed down his arms
for extra thrust.

The pain returned as he put pressure on his bad knee. But it stopped as soon as he found a foot-hold higher up with his good leg. Fear drove him on.

Joe bent down to dig another two steps and then to repeat the pattern,

which worked into a natural rhythm. Bend, hop, rest. Bend, hop, rest. The painful routine became automatic. Bend, hop, rest. Bend, hop, rest.

After about two and a half hours, the slope became much steeper. Joe knew he had to be more careful when he made his hopping movement.

The worst moment came when he rested his weight on the axes. The steeper angle forced him to judge his movements very carefully. He had already nearly fallen a couple of times. As he saved himself, his knee moved painfully.

Joe listened to his sobs and swearing echoing up from the crevasse below.

CHAPTER SIX

Joe was now soaked in sweat and rested his head against the snow to cool down. Quite soon he was shivering again. But when he looked up at the roof, he could see the sun was almost touching him. Glancing down, he saw that he was about two-thirds of the way up the cone of snow.

But the agony wasn't over yet. Joe took another two and a half hours to reach the top, still working to his rhythm of bend, hop and rest.

The angle of the snow cone was even steeper now.

Each hop had to be extra careful so that he didn't fall. Then, as the cone narrowed, the snow got deeper.

Suddenly, his helmet brushed against snow. He was directly below the small hole that had let in the inviting sunbeam. A wave of happiness filled him.

Joe poked out his head. Slowly, painfully, he dragged himself from the crevasse into the beauty of the sunlit peaks. He could hardly believe he had survived. Every muscle ached and he had never felt so tired. Yet he was alive. The magic of the sunbeam had filled him with an energy and courage he had never realised he had.

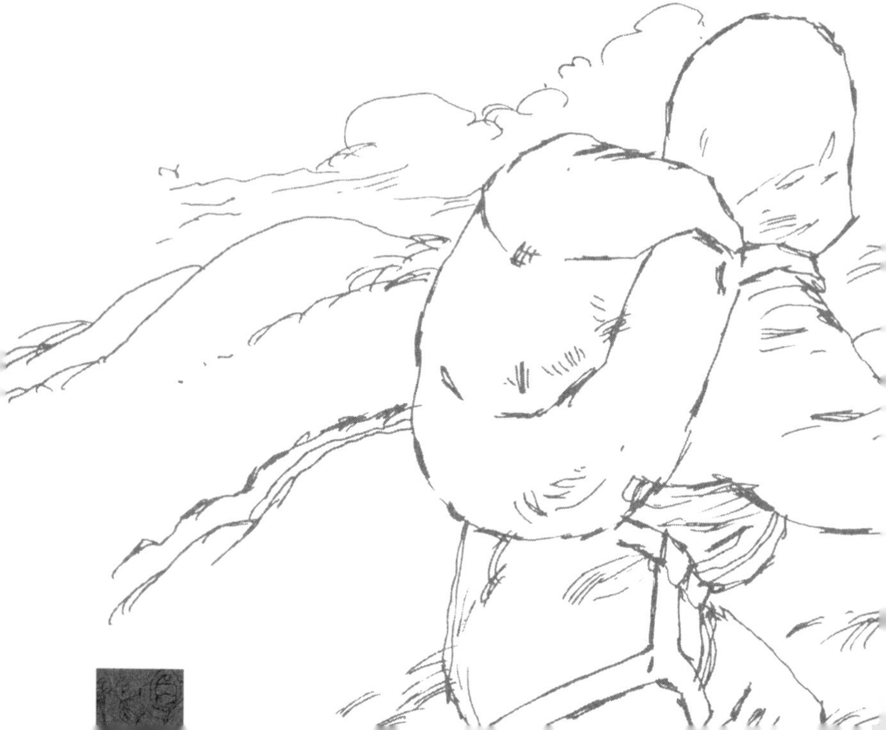

THE SUMMIT

■ CHAPTER ONE

Julie and her climbing partner, Kurt, were very tired indeed. They had been clambering up Broad Peak for seven hours.

The altitude was now over 7,000 metres and they were carrying a lot of equipment.

Broad Peak is in the Karakoram Mountains between China and Pakistan. Other expeditions had also been on the mountain, but Julie and Kurt felt it would be too risky to rely on their tents and food supplies. They could have been destroyed by the weather.

CLIMBING EQUIPMENT

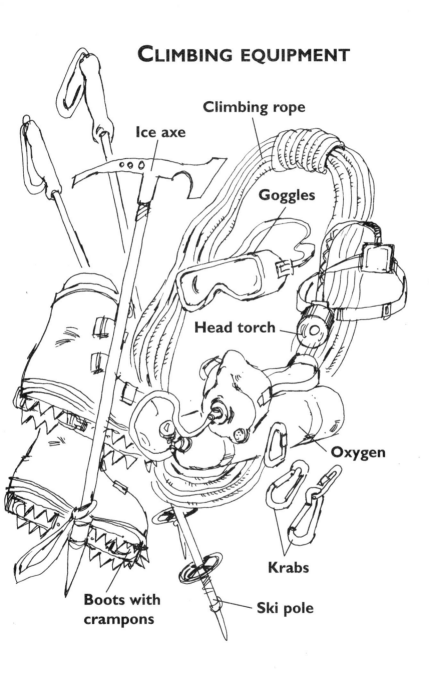

Climbing rope

Ice axe

Goggles

Head torch

Oxygen

Krabs

Boots with
crampons

Ski pole

As a result, Julie and Kurt were carrying everything they needed. Their supplies included a small bivouac tent, sleeping bags, foam mattresses, stove and gas cylinders, pots, food, camera and films, batteries, head torches, spare clothing, ropes, ice axes and various other pieces of equipment.

A modern rucksack weighs over two kilos even when it's empty. In all, Kurt and Julie were carrying at least 45 kilos each. It would have been hard to carry such a weight for seven hours on the flat. But Kurt and Julie were going steeply uphill!

Just after 6.00 pm they glimpsed the small tent that was the next camp. It was high up on a snow slope under a large cliff of ice.

As the light began to fade, Kurt took the lead and they started to zig-zag up the steep slope. Snow began to fall and they were relieved to have found the camp.

But the slow journey seemed to last for ever. Julie was now aching all over. She hoped that Kurt would stop, if only for a moment. But she also knew he couldn't, because it was getting too dark and cold. They had to keep going.

◼ CHAPTER TWO

When it was dark, Kurt took out his head torch. They had decided only to use his. Julie's torch had to be saved for an emergency.

She stepped in Kurt's footsteps just as his feet were leaving them, but the difficult journey was becoming harder. Julie thought the climb would never end. The camp seemed to be as far away as ever.

Suddenly they struck a very deep patch of snow, sinking up to their waists. They managed to struggle out, but Kurt realised he had to go even slower. He had to probe carefully

with a ski stick to find a safe way
forward.

At last they reached the camp.

The next day, Julie and Kurt set up
their own bivouac at 7,400 metres.
They were on a shelf that Kurt had
dug out on the lip of a crevasse.

They then had to wait until the
weather cleared before climbing on

towards the summit of Broad Peak.

At 10.00 am the following morning they were able to get going. They were soon struggling through deep, soft snow. Julie's technique was to take a deep breath and swing her foot with a strong kicking motion into the steep snow slope. But as soon as she put her weight on it, to kick forward with her other leg, it sank deep into the snow. This made the climb frustratingly slow and Julie saw that Kurt was having the same problem.

To keep herself going, Julie picked out a landmark, a small rock further up the slope. She reckoned she would reach the rock in no more than two hundred and forty steps.

'No cheating,' Julie whispered to herself, and began to chant, 'Kick, step up, one and then breathe. Kick, step up, two and then breathe.' At every tenth step, she stopped to rest.

▓ CHAPTER THREE

Julie suddenly realised that grey storm clouds were hanging menacingly above them.

'Keep your mind on the job,' she told herself. 'Don't start to feel sorry for yourself. Just think how lucky you are to be here.'

Julie gazed down at Kurt. He was moving slowly up the slope behind her. She then began to try and take up the tough rhythm of the climb again.

They topped the next ridge just after noon. It was bitterly cold. Their faces were protected by snow goggles

and climbing helmets, but wind-driven
snow can always find tiny areas of
exposed skin.

Julie and Kurt were now at more
than 7,800 metres, but they were still
well over two kilometres from the
summit. They had to find shelter.

Luckily, there was a dip in the snow and they sat close together with their backs to the freezing wind.

Kurt tried to use his lighter to get the stove going, but again and again the flame was blown out. This was deeply depressing. They had fought the snow and wind and ice for hours, helped on by the thought of a hot drink. Now it looked as if they weren't going to get one!

Kurt and Julie took it in turns to try and light the Gaz stove with his lighter. But once their gloves were off the wind numbed their fingers in seconds. They had to stop and put their gloves on again.

CHAPTER FOUR

At last the stove was lit and they began to melt snow for that much-needed hot drink.

Neither Julie nor Kurt could see anything through the snowflakes. They knew, however, that on one side the mountain dropped sharply to the Godwin Austen glacier 300 metres below. The other side dropped even more steeply, over 3,000 metres, into China. They both needed to get back some strength for the final climb to the summit.

Making drinks was a slow process. As they finished one drink, Kurt and

Julie began to melt more snow for the next. Owing to the altitude, each 125 ml of liquid took about twenty minutes to reach boiling point. But they had to drink as much as possible. At this height, the oxygen level in the body is reduced by one-third. That would make it hard for them to push themselves to the limit to make the final climb.

After three hot drinks Julie and Kurt were still feeling very cold. Kurt, in particular, had freezing feet. He knew if he couldn't warm them up he and Julie would have to go back down. He would run the risk of severe frostbite and might have to have his toes cut off if he tried to climb on.

Julie felt deeply disappointed. But she knew that the bad weather meant that their hopes of reaching the summit were getting slimmer all the time.

■ CHAPTER FIVE

Kurt stamped his feet, trying to
exercise his legs, and Julie began to
pray. They had already been driven
down from K2 (the highest mountain
in the Karakoram range) by storms
and that had been bad enough.

Julie was determined to reach the
Broad Peak summit. She was a good
climber and her will was as strong as
her body – if not stronger.

Kurt, however, was the more
experienced climber and had great
reserves of strength. But at the
moment it still looked as if he was
going to have to give up.

Julie wanted to climb the peak for her husband, Terry. He was a mountain photographer and understood how she felt about climbing. He had encouraged her to join international expeditions so that she could really stretch herself. She also wanted to climb the summit for her two children, as well as for the film she and Kurt were making.

Eventually they decided to move round the ridge to get out of the wind. If the gale persisted, that would be another depressing reason for returning to base.

As they reached the other side of the ridge they noticed that the icy wind had dropped.

They were suddenly free to go for the summit.

■ CHAPTER SIX

After an hour and a half of stiff climbing, Julie looked ahead in joy. At last she could see the summit. But it was already 5.00 pm.

On the Chinese side of the mountain the sky was cloudless, but the clouds were beginning to close in on the side facing Pakistan. They were going to have to hurry.

Julie felt very tired. It was her turn to wonder if she could make it. But she knew she had to. She could feel Terry and her children urging her on.

The effort of keeping going at 7,900 metres was very demanding. By

the time Julie was half an hour from
the summit her legs felt so heavy that
they would barely carry her twenty
steps. Was she going to collapse
before she got there?

The thin air, the physical pain and a feeling of hopelessness began to undermine her willpower.

Realising how bad she felt, Kurt set Julie targets to reach. He told her to try and get to the next layer of rock. Then she could take a short rest. After that she must push on to the next obstacle. When she reached it, she could take another rest.

They both continued in this way until they arrived at the foot of the summit. Spurred on by a feeling of intense excitement, they climbed the last six metres.

It was 6.30 pm and the light was beginning to fade as Julie Tullis gazed down at the grey storm clouds over the mountains of Pakistan.

But she felt a real sense of achievement.

Although the weather had been so much against them, they had both made the peak. They had encouraged each other with their different skills and shared the problems.

Julie walked as close to the edge of the summit as she could and held up her ice axe in triumph. The feeling of conquest was overpowering.

Editor's note
Julie and Kurt successfully returned from their expedition to the Broad Peak summit. Julie's book, Clouds From Both Sides, *was published in 1986.*

GLOSSARY

Andes a range of mountains in South America.

avalanche a mass of snow and ice hurtling down a mountainside.

bivouac a camp to rest at night in the open air.

blizzard a blinding storm of wind and snow.

Broad Peak a peak in the Karakoram mountains.

buttress a piece of rock that sticks out and acts as a support.

cone a curved triangular shape, circular and wide at the bottom and pointed at the top.

crevasse a split in a glacier.

Everest the world's highest mountain; it is in the Himalayas.

foothold a place to fix the foot in, a step.

frostbite an injury in a part of the body frozen from being exposed to the cold.

gas cylinder a container to hold gas under pressure.

Gaz stove a make of portable stove with a gas cylinder at the bottom and a cooking ring on the top, used for cooking and boiling water outdoors.

ice axe an axe used by mountain climbers to cut steps in the ice.

Karakoram Mountains a range of mountains between China and Pakistan.

K2 the highest mountain in the Karakoram range.

knots the speed of wind is measured in knots.

landmark any obvious object to serve as a guide.

oxygen bottle a container for oxygen.

oxygen mask a covering for the nose and mouth to allow someone to breathe extra oxygen.

ridge a long narrow line of mountaintops.

shaft a beam of light.

shelf a ledge of rock.

ski stick a stick or pole to push yourself along and help you balance when skiing.

snow goggles glasses for protecting the eyes against the glare of sunlight bouncing off snow.

summit the top of a mountain.

suspended hanging in space.

valve a device to regulate the flow of something.

vertical in an upright position.

91

Other titles in this series

Daring Escapes

Luis knew the main battle was raging in the valley and it would be crazy to go down there.
The bullets thudded around the rocks.
Luis realised he could be hit at any moment.

Read Daring Escapes and find out how ordinary people cheated death in wartime.

Football Heroes

Cantona always looked very cool. He wore his shirt collar casually turned up and his face showed no interest in what was going on around him. That, of course, was misleading; in fact, he was totally focused.

Read Football Heroes and find out about the thrilling careers of some of the giants of football.

Terror at Sea

*Jacques and Frédéric thought they might be able
to escape – that is, unless one of them got wounded.
At the first sign of blood the sharks
would attack them both.*

*Read Terror at Sea and find out about narrow
escapes from a watery grave.*